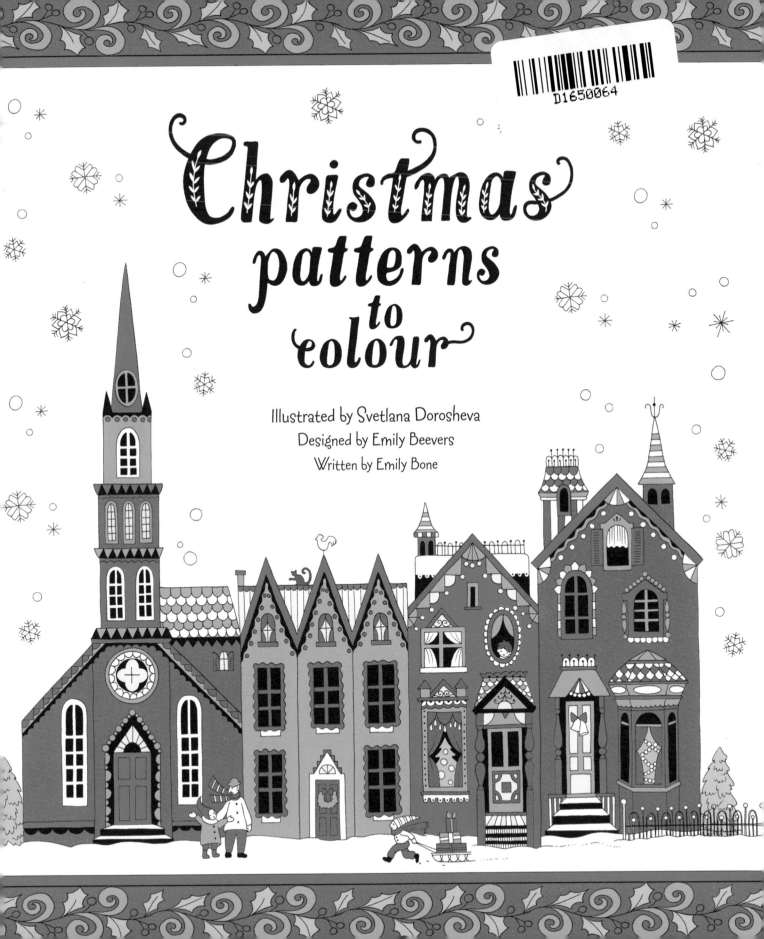

Christmas patterns to colour

Illustrated by Svetlana Dorosheva

Designed by Emily Beevers

Written by Emily Bone

The Christmas festival

Christmas is a festival held every year to celebrate the birth of Jesus, who Christians believe is the son of God. Christmas is celebrated on December 24th or 25th in most countries, but on January 7th in Russia. The four weeks leading up to Christmas are known as Advent.

There are many traditions around the Christmas period, including giving gifts wrapped in colourful, patterned paper, gathering together for huge feasts, and decorating a Christmas tree. Traditional Christmas colours are green, red, silver and gold.

Christmas fir trees became popular around 200 years ago, when Prince Albert, the German husband of the British Queen Victoria, introduced this tradition from Germany.

Traditional decorations, such as baubles and tinsel, were originally made from glass and silver.

Nutcracker dolls are traditional German dolls.

An angel or star usually goes on the top of a Christmas tree. These are part of the Christmas Nativity story (see opposite).

Christmas candles

Candles are popular Christmas symbols. In an Advent wreath, candles sit in a circle of pine or holly branches. The candle in the middle is lit on Christmas Day.

Father Christmas delivers presents on a sleigh pulled by flying reindeer.

Father Christmas

Father Christmas, or Santa Claus, is said to deliver presents to well-behaved children on Christmas Eve. He is based on Saint Nicholas, who lived nearly 2,000 years ago and was known for giving lots of gifts.

The Nativity

The Nativity is the story of the birth of Jesus in a stable in Bethlehem as told in the Bible. Many Christmas symbols, such as the Star of Bethlehem and angels, come from the Nativity story.

The Star of Bethlehem was a bright star that appeared on the night Jesus was born.

Angels announced the birth of the baby Jesus.

Three Kings followed the star from faraway lands to visit Jesus.

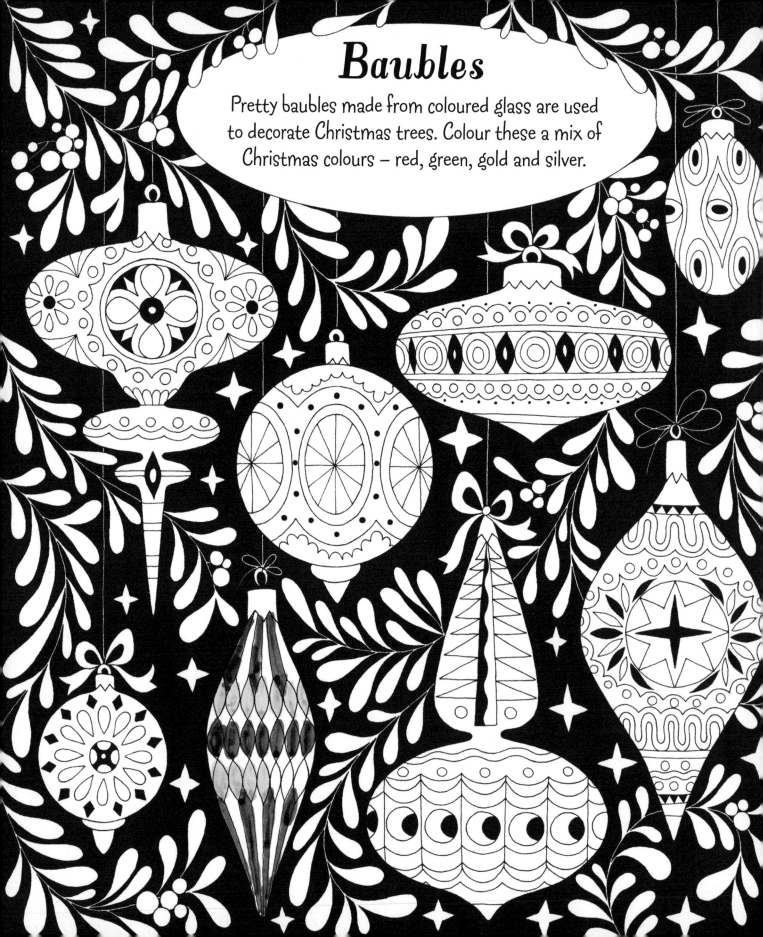

Baubles

Pretty baubles made from coloured glass are used to decorate Christmas trees. Colour these a mix of Christmas colours – red, green, gold and silver.

Christmas treats

Jars full of cookies and other sweet treats are traditionally given as gifts at Christmas. Candy canes are peppermint-flavoured sticks – often coloured red or green and white.

Christmas angels

In the Nativity story, winged angels announce baby Jesus's birth. They're now popular Christmas ornaments and sometimes sit on the top of a Christmas tree.

Christmas Eve

Christmas trees

Christmas gifts

Giving gifts at Christmas is an important and ancient tradition. In the Nativity story, the Three Kings brought gifts to Jesus in Bethlehem to celebrate his birth. Nowadays, people wrap their gifts in colourful wrapping paper.

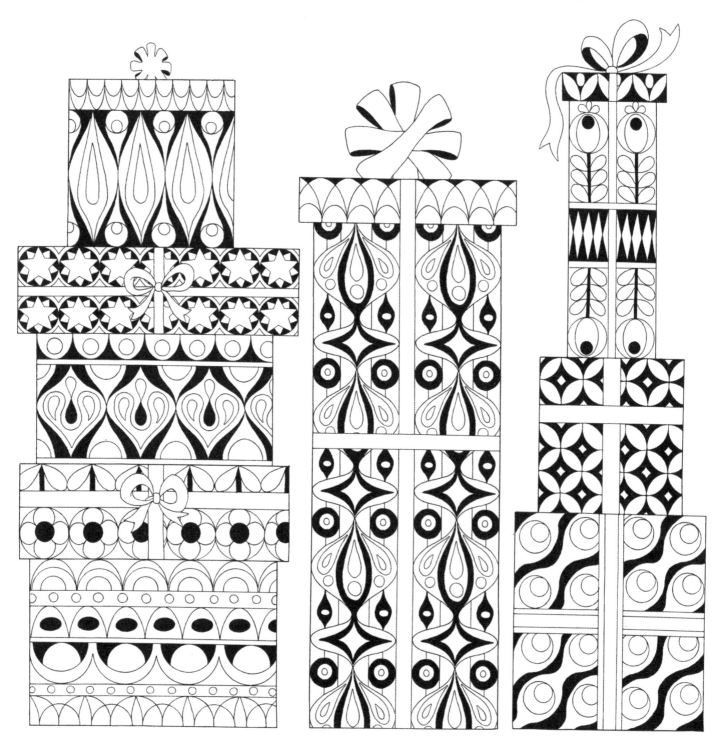

Bells and candles

Many people go to a Christmas Day church service.
Traditionally, bells ring out on Christmas morning
to call people to church.

Christmas stockings

Children hang up stockings on Christmas Eve, ready for
Father Christmas to fill them with gifts.

The Christmas toyshop

Christmas patterns

Usborne Quicklinks

For links to websites where you can find out more about traditional Christmas decorations, symbols and stories, and the history of Christmas celebrations, go to the Usborne Quicklinks website at usborne.com/Quicklinks and enter the keywords 'Christmas patterns'. Please follow the internet safety guidelines at the Usborne Quicklinks website.

First published in 2017 by Usborne Publishing, 83-85 Saffron Hill, London EC1N 8RT, UK. usborne.com Copyright © 2017 Usborne Publishing Ltd. The name Usborne and the Balloon logo are Trade Marks of Usborne Publishing Ltd. All rights reserved. No part of this publication may be reproduced, stored in a retrieval system or transmitted in any form or by any means without the prior permission of Usborne Publishing Ltd. UKE.